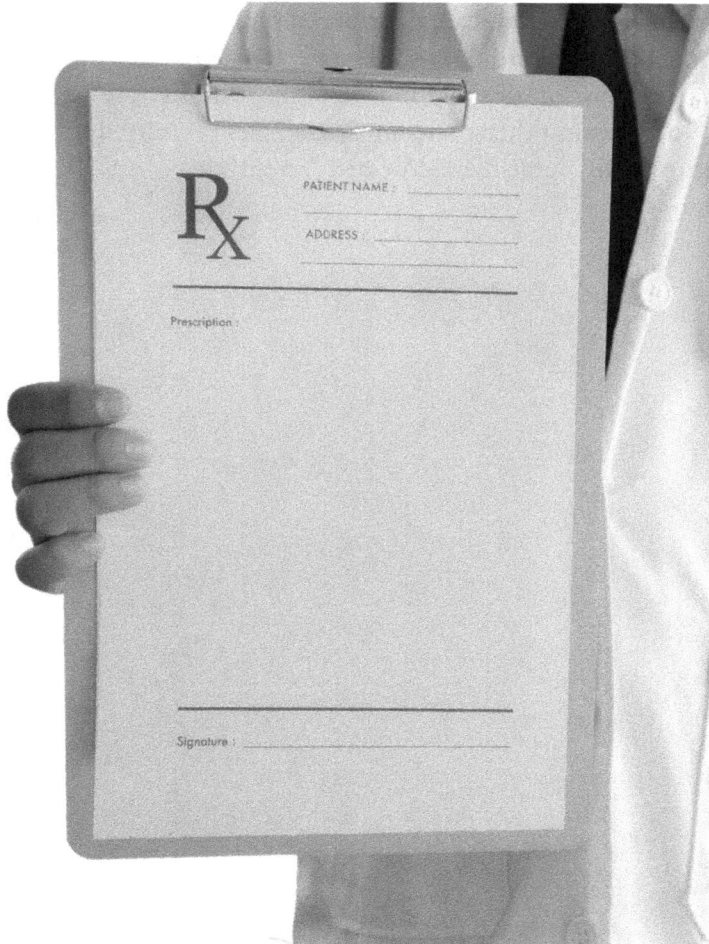

The Writing Rx Workbook

Guided Activities in Expressive Writing

Ann Eichenmuller

HighTide
Publications, Inc.

Deltaville, Virginia

High Tide Publications, Inc.
1000 Bland Point
Deltaville, Virginia 23043
www.hightidepublications.com

First Edition

ISBN: 978-1-945990-87-8

Table of Contents

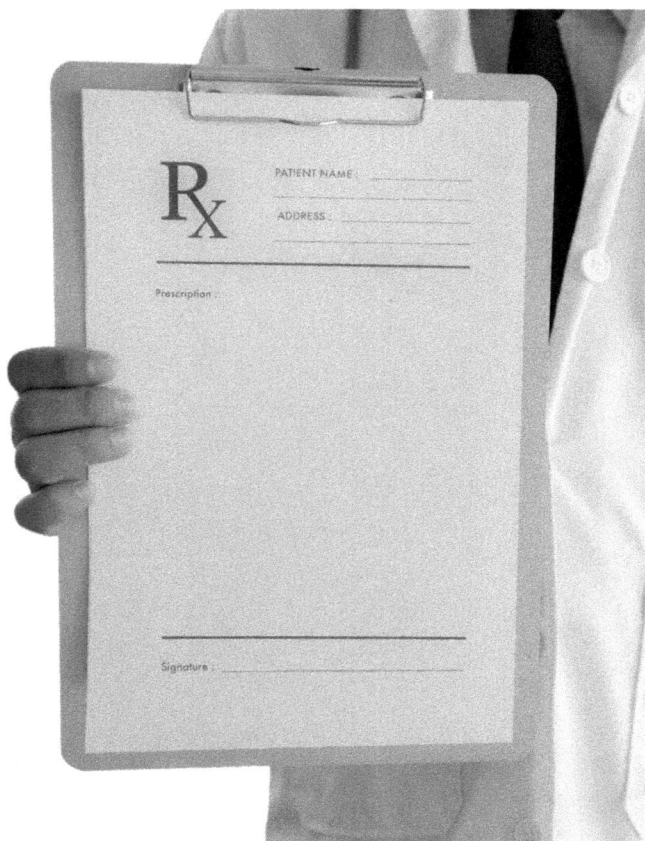

Author's Note

In *The Writing Rx,* I summarize current research documenting the physical and mental health benefits of expressive writing and provide some general guidance on what to write and how to write it. But taking pen in hand or sitting in front of a keyboard can be a little dauting, especially if it isn't something you are used to doing. Early on, readers asked for additional resources to walk them through some of the writing processes discussed in *The Writing Rx,* and in answer this workbook was created.

Ideally, the activities included here should be used in conjunction with *The Writing Rx.* It is important to understand why we need to write and what the research says about writing, health, and happiness. That is not information you can get simply from trying out activities. To reap the greatest benefit from the exercises in this book, you need to get the backstory.

If you have read *The Writing Rx* and want to incorporate writing in your everyday life, this workbook gives you a structured, step-by-step place to start. But please—do not feel you have to begin on page one and try every activity in order. All of these pages are reproducible for personal use, so you can use each page once or a hundred times, or you can skip an exercise altogether.

Never think that your self-expression should be limited by these exercises. They are a launching pad for your creativity. As long as you think deeply about what you write and focus on learning and growing from the experience, whatever you do will have positive results. The most important step is just getting started, so get out your pen, choose an activity, and write.

You'll be glad you did.

Ann Eichenmuller

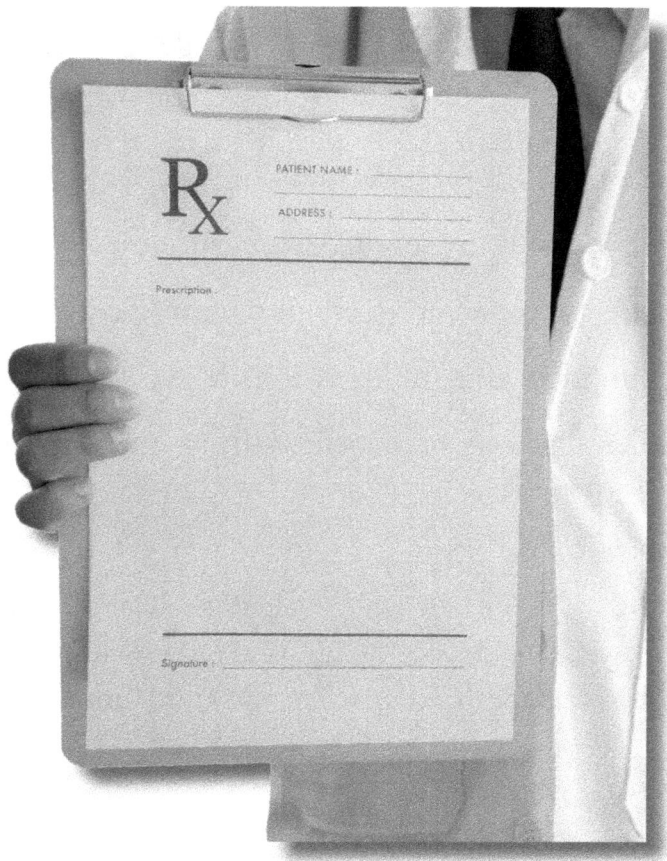

Journaling

The List Journal

Weekly Gratitude Calendar

Diary Journal

Reflective Journal Starters

Journal Starters

Free Writing

Extended Reflective Response

Journaling is short, expressive writing meant to be done at regular intervals. You can choose to write once a week, several times a week, or every day.

When you first start out, it is a good idea to set aside specific days and times to journal so that you can develop a routine. You need to give yourself a minimum of five to ten minutes of uninterrupted time to write, though fifteen minutes or more is optimal.

Choose a place to write that will be free from distractions. The quality of your experience is directly related to the quality of the time you invest.

There are no hard and fast rules to journaling. Your entries can be as short as a sentence or two and as much as a page or more in length. Don't worry about spelling and grammar. This is writing by you and for you—no one else will see it. Think deeply. Write honestly.

Reflect on your words. They are a physical manifestation of your thoughts and feelings. This makes them real, valid, and important—just like their writer.

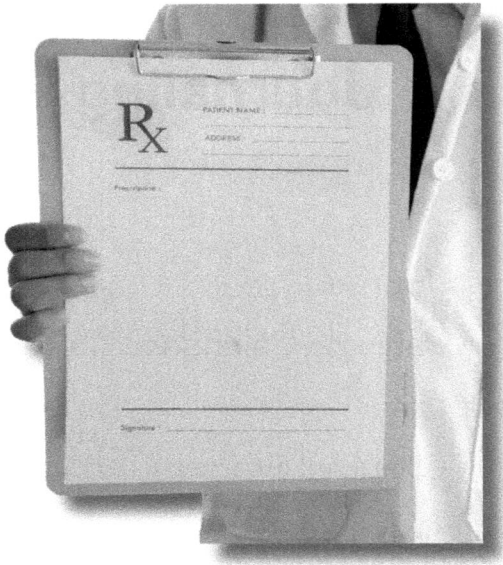

The List Journal

Choose one of the list topics below.

• What I love about my spouse/significant other

• What I am appreciate most about my son/daughter

• What I am most grateful for in my life

• How I have grown or benefited from an otherwise difficult experience

Write three to five responses that fit the topic you've chosen. Explain why each item on your list is important to you. Try to go beyond superficial answers and think about what is truly meaningful.

_____

_____

_____

_____

_____

_____

_____

How did writing this list make you feel? Why?

_____

_____

_____

_____

_____

Weekly Gratitude Calendar 1

Write three to five sentences each day in response to the topic.

Sunday Who is one person you are grateful for in your life, and why?	
Monday Tell about one act of kindness you've seen in the last week.	
Tuesday Describe one memory that you treasure most.	
Wednesday What one quality do you value most about yourself? Why?	
Thursday Name someone from your past you'd like to go back and thank and explain why.	
Friday What is one thing someone did for you this week?	
Saturday What is the most meaningful gift you've ever received?	

Weekly Gratitude Calendar 2

Write three to five sentences each day in response to the topic.

Sunday What happened today that made you smile?	
Monday Think of someone you care about and tell what he/she means to you.	
Tuesday What is one basic need that you are grateful is being met? Why?	
Wednesday Tell about a time someone surprised you by doing something nice.	
Thursday Tell about one place you love to be.	
Friday What is one thing you would like to do for someone else?	
Saturday What is one challenge you've overcome?	

Weekly Gratitude Calendar 3

Write three to five sentences each day in response to the topic.

Sunday Tell about a favorite childhood memory.	
Monday Describe one person you are grateful you know or knew.	
Tuesday Tell about one positive thing that happened to you last week.	
Wednesday What is one thing in your life you are proud you have done? Why?	
Thursday What is one way someone has shown they care about you?	
Friday Tell about a time someone did something for you without being asked.	
Saturday Describe an activity that brings you joy.	

Weekly Gratitude Calendar #4

Write three to five sentences each day in response to the topic.

Sunday Tell about an event you are grateful you experienced.	
Monday What is one thing you are grateful your parents taught you?	
Tuesday Tell about one positive thing that came out of a difficult experience.	
Wednesday Describe one goal in your life that you have met.	
Thursday Describe a possession you own that holds special significance.	
Friday Tell about one thing you are glad you did this week.	
Saturday Describe a goal or hope you have for the future.	

Diary Journal

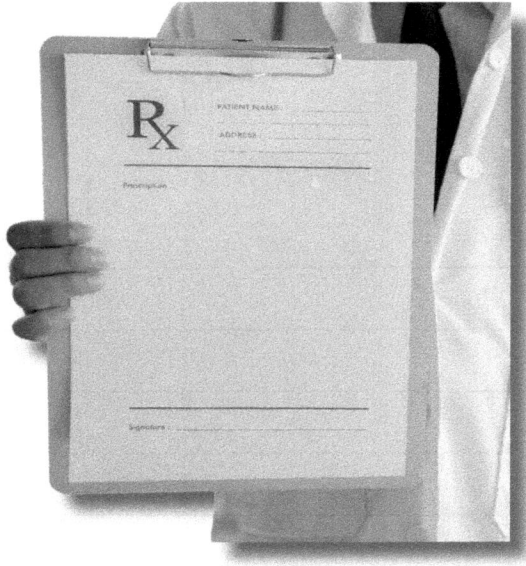

Set aside ten minutes at the end of each day, four to seven times a week.

Look over the sentence starters below while you think about the events of the day. Does one fit what you have experienced in the past twenty-four hours? If so, use that as your starter. If not, create a sentence starter of your own that best reflects what has happened in your life today.

Sentence Starters:

- I felt proud of myself today when….

- Today I dealt with stress from….

- The greatest challenge I faced today was….

- Something unexpected happened when….

- I regret that today I….

- Today I feel _____ because….

- I made the best of a difficult situation today by….

- I am grateful today that….

Write for a minimum of five to ten minutes about the topic you chose. If you have started keeping a dedicated journal, date and write your response there. If not, use the space on the next page.

Date:_____

_____

_____

_____

_____

_____

_____

_____

_____

Read over your journal entry. How do you feel now about the day?

_____

_____

_____

_____

Is there anything you'd like to keep in mind for tomorrow?

_____

_____

_____

_____

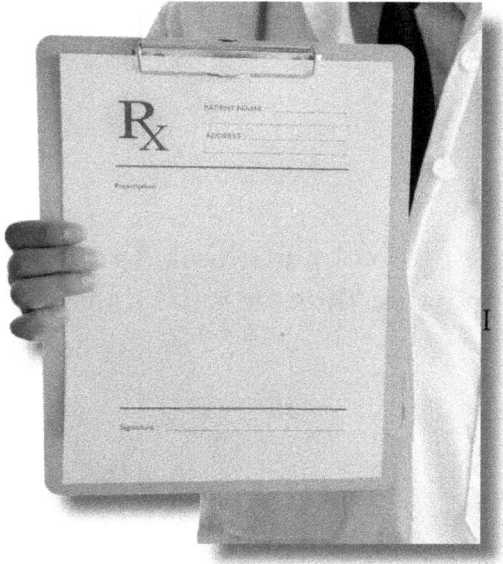

Reflective Journal Starters

Choose one of these topics and think, write, and reflect for fifteen minutes, three or more times each week.

If I could change one thing about myself, I would _____

_____

_____

_____

_____

If I weren't afraid, I'd like to _____

_____

_____

_____

My worst fear is _____

_____

_____

_____

If I could only keep one possession, it would be_____

_____

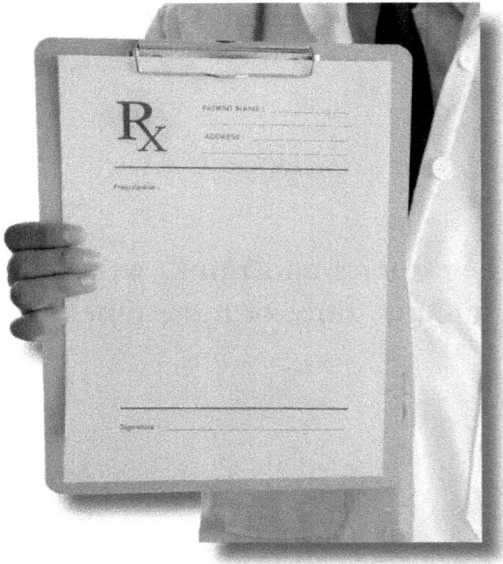

Journal Starters

Choose one of these topics and think, write, and reflect for fifteen minutes, three or more times each week.

_____

My most embarrassing moment was _____

_____

_____

_____

The thing I admire most about my husband/wife/significant other is_____

_____

_____

_____

The one place I'd like to see before I die is_____

_____

_____

_____

The first person I'd like to see in heaven is_____

Free Writing

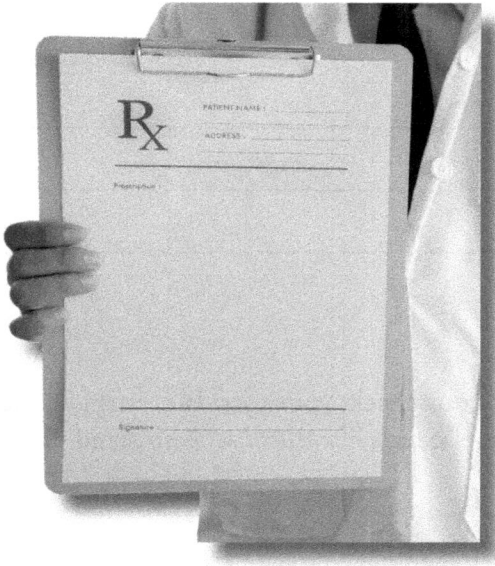

Choose one of the objects from the list below that has some meaning or connection to your past.

- A baby blanket
- A skateboard
- A pet collar
- A dried corsage
- A pair of women's gloves
- A children's backyard swing set
- A diary
- A stuffed animal
- A baseball/softball glove

Why did you choose this object? What significance does it have for you?

_____

_____

_____

_____

_____

Close your eyes and visualize the object you chose as it exists/existed in your own life.

- Think of the object's color, its shape, its edges, and its curves. List as many words and phrases as you can in the space below to describe the object's appearance.

_____

_____

_____

_____

Does its appearance remind you of anything else?

_____

_____

_____

Engage your other senses.

- Imagine that you can touch it with your lips, the bare skin of your cheek, your toes. Is it warm or cool? Run some bit of it between your fingers, feel the texture. What else feels like this? List words and phrases to describe how it feels.

_____

_____

_____

_____

Breathe it in. What do you smell? How does it make you feel?

_____

_____

_____

_____

Taste it. Is it salty, sweet, bitter, sharp?

_____

_____

Be still and listen. Are there any sounds associated with this object in your memory? What do you hear?

_____

_____

Read over your free writing. What is the overall mood or tone of what you have written?

_____

_____

_____

This exercise can be done again and again using an object, place, or a person from your own life.

A free-write can serve as the basis for a poem, a paragraph, an essay, and even a memoir. If this exercise was meaningful for you, consider coming back to it at a later time and using it as the starting point for another piece of writing.

Extended Reflective Response

Exercise 1 - Think about your happiest day. Write a paragraph describing this event, focusing on using positive words that capture your joy. As you write, take the time to think about what happened, and how and why it made you feel the way it did.

_____

_____

_____

_____

_____

_____

_____

_____

_____

_____

_____

_____

_____

_____

_____

_____

How do you feel after writing about this incident?

_____

_____

_____

_____

Exercise 2 - Think about an emotional event or incident in the past that troubled, upset, or hurt you deeply. Write a paragraph describing this event. As you write, take the time to think about what happened, why it was so upsetting or hurtful, and how and why it made you feel the way it did.

_____

_____

_____

_____

_____

_____

_____

_____

_____

_____

_____

_____

How do you feel after writing about this incident? How can thinking about what happened make you a happier or stronger person?

_____

_____

_____

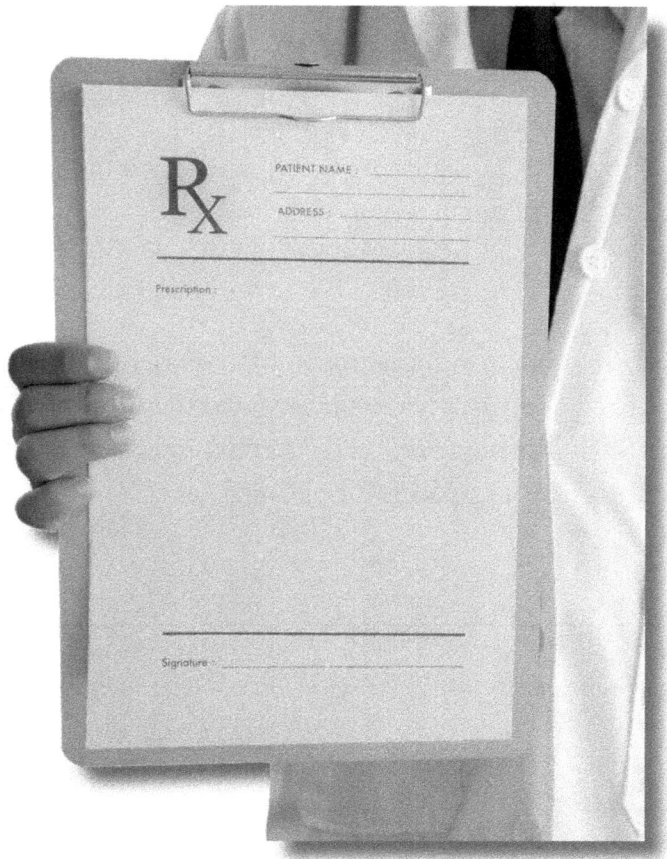

Letter Writing

The Letter to God

The Gratitude Letter

The I'm Sorry Letter

The Unfinished Business Letter

The Understanding Letter

The Letter to the Future

L etters are structured, focused pieces of writing addressed to another person. They require organization and purpose. Because they are written with someone else in mind, they require the writer to consider the perspective of someone other than himself, even if the intended reader never receives them.

The letters in this section are not meant to be sent. Rather, they provide an opportunity for self-awareness and understanding. They can be useful in clarifying your thoughts and feelings if you are planning for a difficult conversation. They are especially meaningful in achieving a sense of closure if physical two-way contact is impossible because of distance, serious illness, or death.

Rx

Strengthing
Spirit

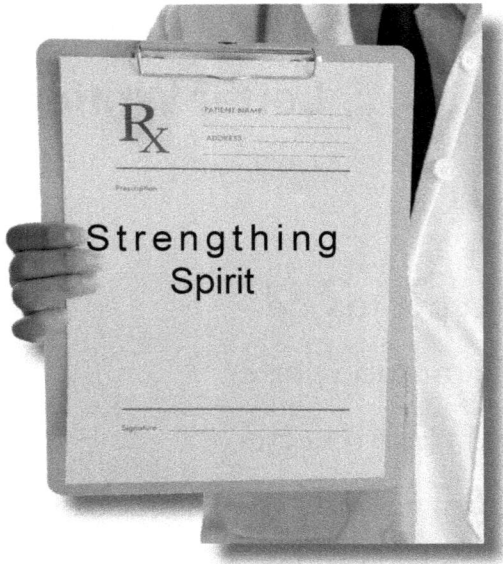

The Letter to God

Think about what God means to you and how He has provided for you. List the most important gifts God has given you. (Examples: material needs, relationships in your life, physical or spiritual healing.)

_____

_____

_____

_____

_____

_____

_____

_____

Choose one of these gifts and describe the context in which it was given.

_____

_____

_____

_____

_____

_____

_____

_____

How did you feel when you received this gift?

_____

_____

_____

_____

In what way has this gift impacted your life?

_____

_____

_____

_____

Writing: *Now write a letter of thanks to God for something He has done for you. Share how much His gift has meant to you and focus on how it has changed or enriched your life.*

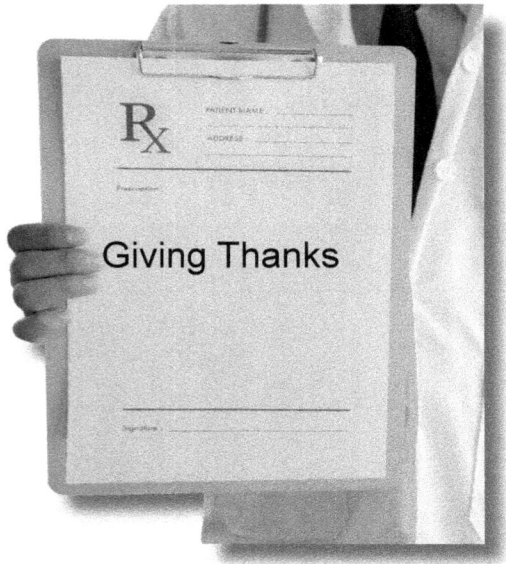

The Gratitude Letter

Giving Thanks

Think of a gift you have received that meant a lot to you. It could be an object, a skill or lesson you were taught, or an action that inspired you or made you happy. Who gave you this gift? _____

In three or four sentences, describe the gift.

_____

_____

_____

_____

_____

_____

What made this gift so meaningful to you?

_____

_____

_____

_____

_____

_____

How did you feel when you received this gift?

_____

_____

_____

_____

In what way did this gift impact or influence your life?

_____

_____

_____

_____

Writing: *Now write a letter of appreciation for a gift you have been given. As you write, think about the emotions you want to convey and the way you hope your reader will feel as he or she reads the letter.*

The I'm Sorry Letter

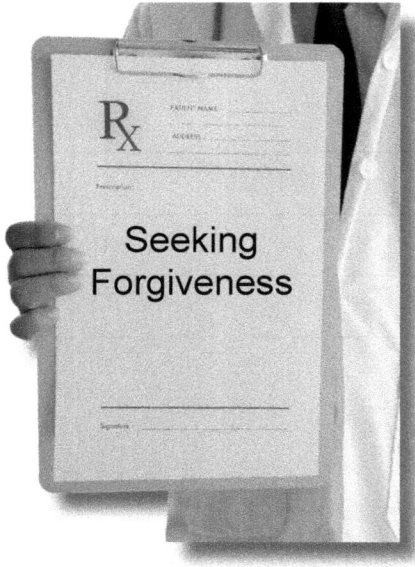

Seeking Forgiveness

Name someone you have hurt or disappointed.

_____

In just two or three sentences, summarize what you did.

_____

_____

_____

_____

Why did you behave this way?

_____

_____

_____

_____

How do you think it made the person feel?

_____

_____

_____

_____

Is there anything you wish you had said or done differently at the time?

_____

_____

_____

What would you most like this person to know now about what happened and how it has affected you?

_____

_____

_____

What do you think it would take for this person to forgive you?

_____

_____

_____

Writing: *Now write a letter to the person you hurt, upset, or disappointed. Clearly state what you did wrong and what the consequences have been for both of you. Ask for forgiveness, and, if possible, tell what you can do to make amends.*

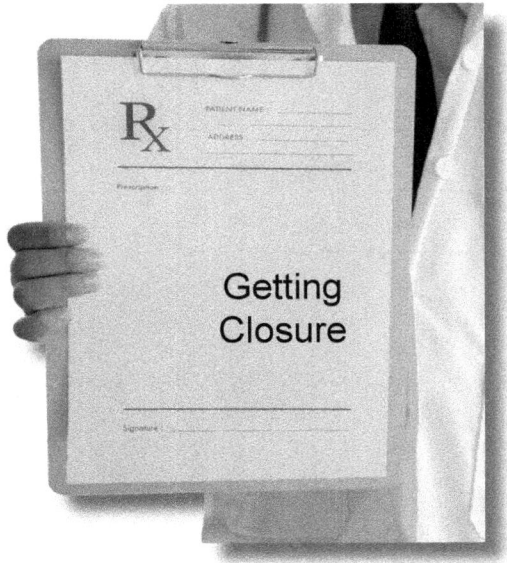

The Unfinished Business Letter

Getting Closure

Name a person from your past that upset or hurt you.

_____

In just two or three sentences, summarize what he or she did.

_____

_____

_____

_____

_____

How did this make you feel?

_____

_____

_____

Why do you think the person behaved this way?

_____

_____

_____

Is there anything you wish you had said or done differently at the time?

_____

_____

_____

What would you most like this person to know now about what happened and how it affected you?

_____

_____

What would it take for you to be able to forgive this person? How might forgiving benefit you?

_____

_____

Writing: *Now write a letter to the person who upset or hurt you. Try not to focus on how "wrong" or cruel the other person was. When you describe how you felt, go beyond surface reactions and concentrate on your deepest feelings. Think about what hurt you the most—words, actions, or unfulfilled expectations? If you share any blame, accept it. Be specific and clear about what you would want to get from this person now.*

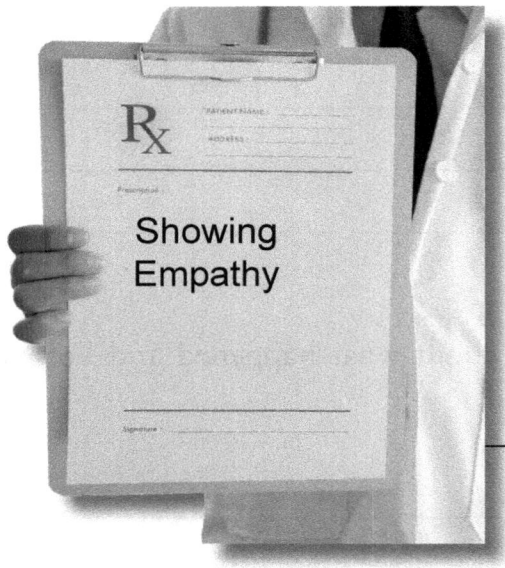

The Understanding Letter

Rx

Showing
Empathy

Name someone you know who is going through a difficult time.

_____

In just two or three sentences, summarize the problem he or she is experiencing.

_____

_____

_____

_____

_____

_____

How would you feel if you were in a similar situation?

_____

_____

_____

If you were in this person's place, what would you need from other people? What words would you most want to hear?

_____

_____

_____

_____

Is there anything in your own life that you could share to show you understand?

_____

_____

_____

_____

Is there anything more you could do to help?

_____

_____

_____

_____

Writing: *Now write a letter to a person dealing with a difficult situation. Let them know you feel empathy for them. Do not preach or express disapproval for how they are handling things, but instead focus on communicating caring, acceptance, and encouragement.*

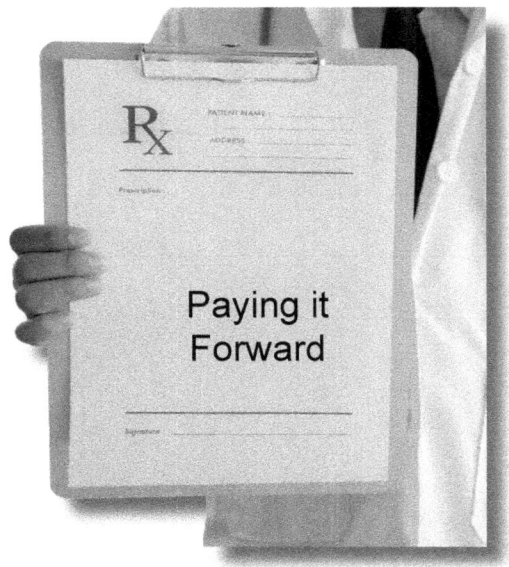

The Letter to the Future

Paying it
Forward

Think of a time or event in the future that will be important to someone in your life. (Examples: a graduation, wedding, birth of a child) Name the event and the persons in your life who will be involved.

_____, _____,

_____, _____

In just two or three sentences, describe the event.

_____

_____

_____

_____

_____

_____

How do you think you will feel if you are able to be there?

_____

_____

_____

What emotions do you hope the person involved will experience?

_____

_____

_____

What advice or wisdom can you share from your own experience that might be meaningful to the person involved?

_____

_____

_____

_____

_____

What would you like to see happen in this person's future as a result of the event?

_____

_____

_____

Writing: _Now write a letter to be given at a future event to someone important in your life. Share your appreciation for their role in your life. Focus on what your reader needs or wants at this future point in life and offer your support and encouragement._

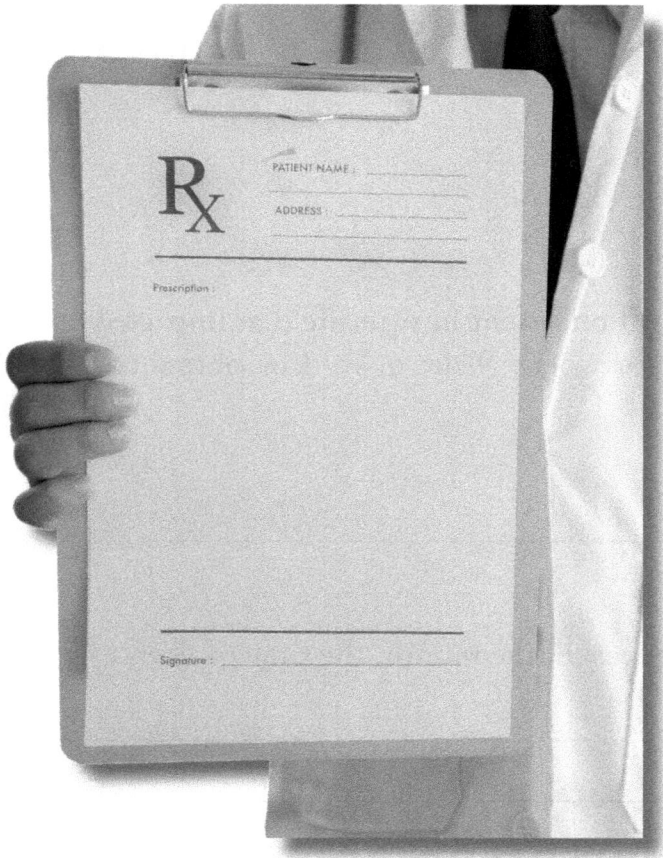

Memoir

The stories about your Life

not

The story of your Life

Amemoir is a written account of a meaningful experience from one's past. It can be a single incident or event, or it can cover a specific time period, such as the Vietnam War, or a stage of one's life, like adolescence. Writing about the past gives us a chance to reflect on where we have been and to think about where we hope to go. With distance from an event comes an opportunity to look at it more closely and to understand it more clearly.

We can write our memoirs for ourselves alone, but many people choose to give their memoirs as gifts to children and grandchildren. Think how valuable such as gift would be to you, especially if you have lost loved ones without ever truly hearing "their story."

Whether you choose to share your memoir or not, the process is the same. Remember to write honestly, to reflect on what you've experienced, and to focus on using your writing as a tool for self-understanding and personal growth.

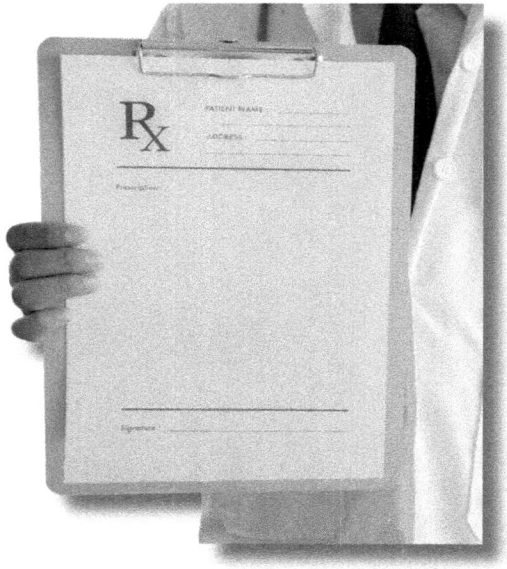

Memoir

Think about one event in your life that impacted you, for better or for worse. Write a word or phrase naming the memory.

_____

When did the event happen? What was the season, the month, the time of day?

_____

_____

_____

Where did the event happen?

_____

Imagine you are there again. What would you see, smell, and hear?

_____

_____

_____

What colors stand out to you?

_____

_____

How old were you? _____

What did you look like?

_____

_____

How were you different then from the person you are today?

_____

_____

_____

_____

Who else was involved in this experience? Write their names below. Describe them. (For each person, think about his or her most distinctive physical and emotional features. Picture the clothing the person wore and visualize the hairstyle and jewelry. Use your senses—did the person use after shave or perfume?)

Name_____Description _____

_____

_____

Name_____Description _____

_____

_____

Name_____Description _____

_____

_____

What were you doing before the event or incident began?

_____

_____

Write a paragraph summarizing the experience. Include what you said and did as well as what others said and did.

_____

_____

_____

_____

_____

_____

_____

Set a timer, and for five minutes tell the story aloud as if you were talking to a friend, without looking at what you have written. Did you fill in details while talking that you did not include in your writing? Jot down these extra details in the margins.

- How did this experience from your past change or impact your life?

_____

_____

_____

_____

- Did it change anyone else's life, and if so, how?

_____

_____

_____

Based on what you have written, why was this event important to you—what did you gain or lose by living it?

_____

_____

_____

_____

_____

Writing: *Now rewrite your memory of the event, being as specific, detailed, and descriptive as you can. Use the same kind of language you used when you were speaking and include your feelings at the time. Stay as close to the truth of your memory as possible. Set a goal of two to three pages.*

Poetry

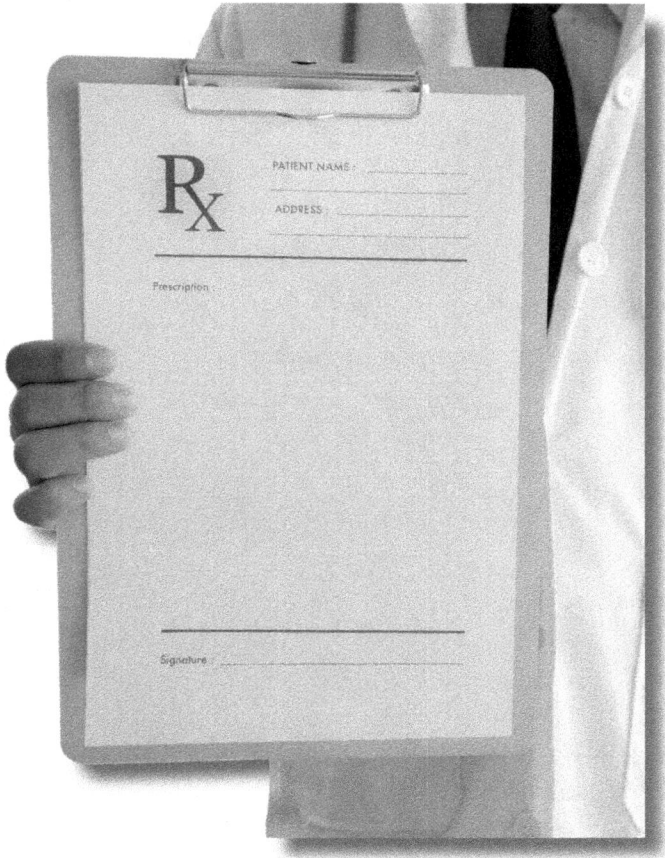

The Diamante or Diamond Poem

The Haiku

Rhyming Poems

The Acrostic Poem

Free Verse

Poems capture the essence of an experience. Because they are shorter than other types of writing, the choice of each word and even where it appears on a page can take on greater importance. There are so many different forms of poetry that a writer has unparalleled freedom—a poem can be rhyming or unrhymed, use punctuation or not, be detailed or sparing, tackle global issues or simply describe a single snowflake. This flexibility makes poetry a perfect vehicle for expressive writing.

What follows are a series of exercises designed around short, easy-to-write poetic forms. If structure isn't for you, skip to the free verse poetry and experiment with your own style and form. The goal, as with all of the writing in the book, is self-expression and reflection.

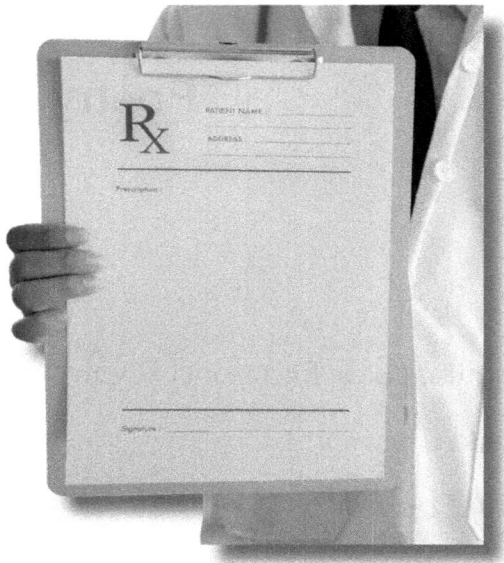

The Diamante or Diamond Poem

love

warm, soft

hugging, touching, feeling

to have and to hold, to hurt and to cast away

blaming, resenting, accusing

icy sharp

hate

The diamante is a seven-line poem in the shape of a diamond. It usually describes two contrasting or conflicting ideas and does not use rhyme. The diamante follows this basic pattern:

Line 1: Beginning subject

Line 2: Two describing words about line 1

Line 3: Three doing words about line 1 ending with ing

Line 4: A short phrase about line 1, a short phrase about line 7

Line 5: Three doing words about line 7

Line 6: Two describing words about line 7

Line 7: End subject

Because it examines opposites, it is a useful form for looking at tension between two areas in your own life. Some examples of common tensions for most people might include desire/duty, hope/despair, youth/age, relationship/independence, take/give, husband/wife, responsibility/freedom, work/leisure, love/hate, bitterness/forgiveness.

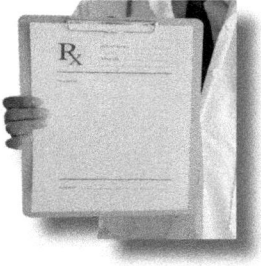

Brainstorming: *Choose a pair of words from the previous page or make up your own. Write one of the words at the top of each circle below from the list of the common opposites on the previous page, or make up your own.*

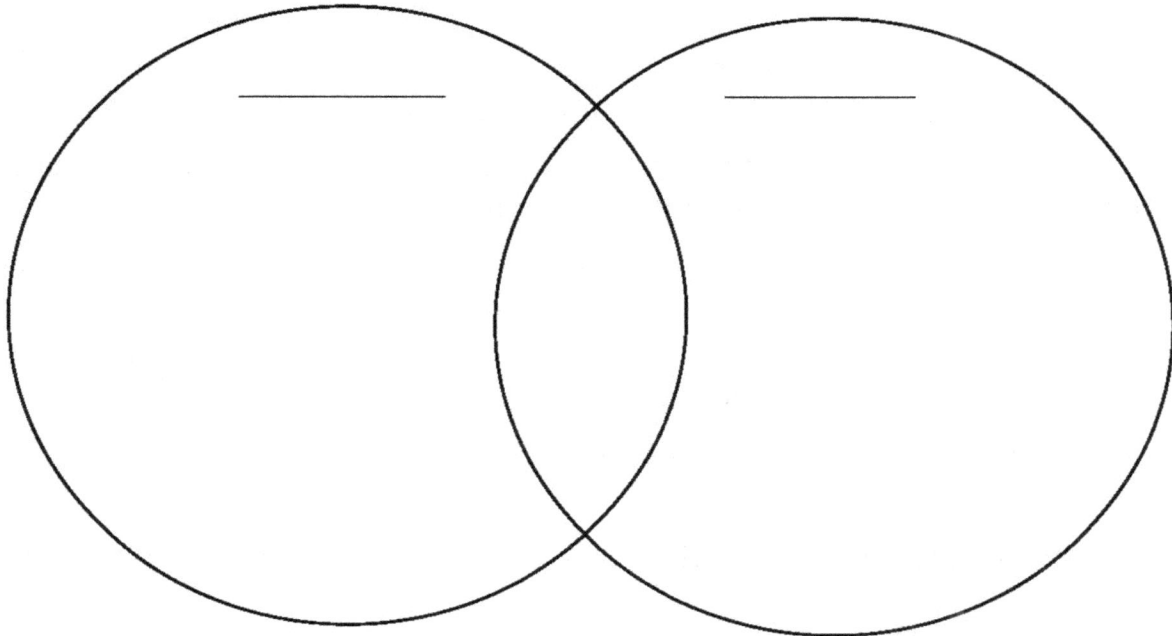

What words or phrases come to mind when you think of each word? Are there any smells or sounds associated with these words? Write your thoughts in the appropriate circle.

Are there any objects or places that remind you of each word? Add those to your circles.

Is there anything the two topics have in common? If so, put those words in the overlapping area.

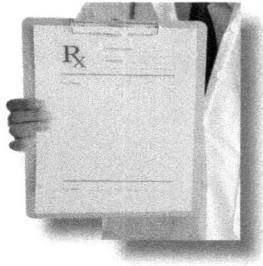

Writing:

1. Write the topic of your first circle on the top line of the diamante form at the bottom of this page.

2. Read over your brainstorming. Choose the two strongest descriptive words and write those on line two.

3. Look for three words in the first circle that can describe something you do. (Examples: kiss, hug, struggle.) Add an -ing to each word and fill in line three.

4. Choose a phrase from your first circle, or write a phrase that summarizes what your first circle is saying. Write it in the first section of line four.

5. Choose a phrase from your second circle or write a phrase that summarizes what your second circle is saying. Write it in the end section of line four.

6. Look for three words in the second circle that can describe something you do. Add an -ing to each word and fill in line five.

7. Choose the two strongest descriptive words from your second circle and write those on line six.

8. Write the topic of your second circle on the last line. Your diamante is complete!

_____

_____, _____

_____, _____, _____

_____, _____

_____, _____, _____

_____, _____

_____

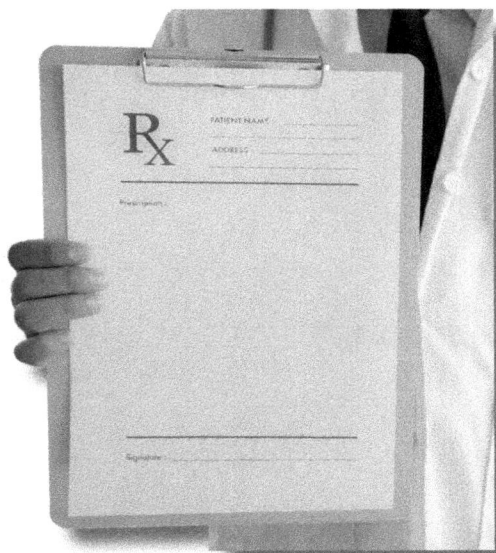

The Haiku

Leaves softly falling

Slow waltz of color and light

Into earth's embrace

A haiku is a short Japanese poetic form. It is meant to capture a single image or moment in time and often focuses on nature. A haiku has only three lines, with a set syllable count (or number of beats) of 5-7-5.* This exercise works best if you are writing about a place and time that you are experiencing, but these can also be written about a moment you clearly remember.

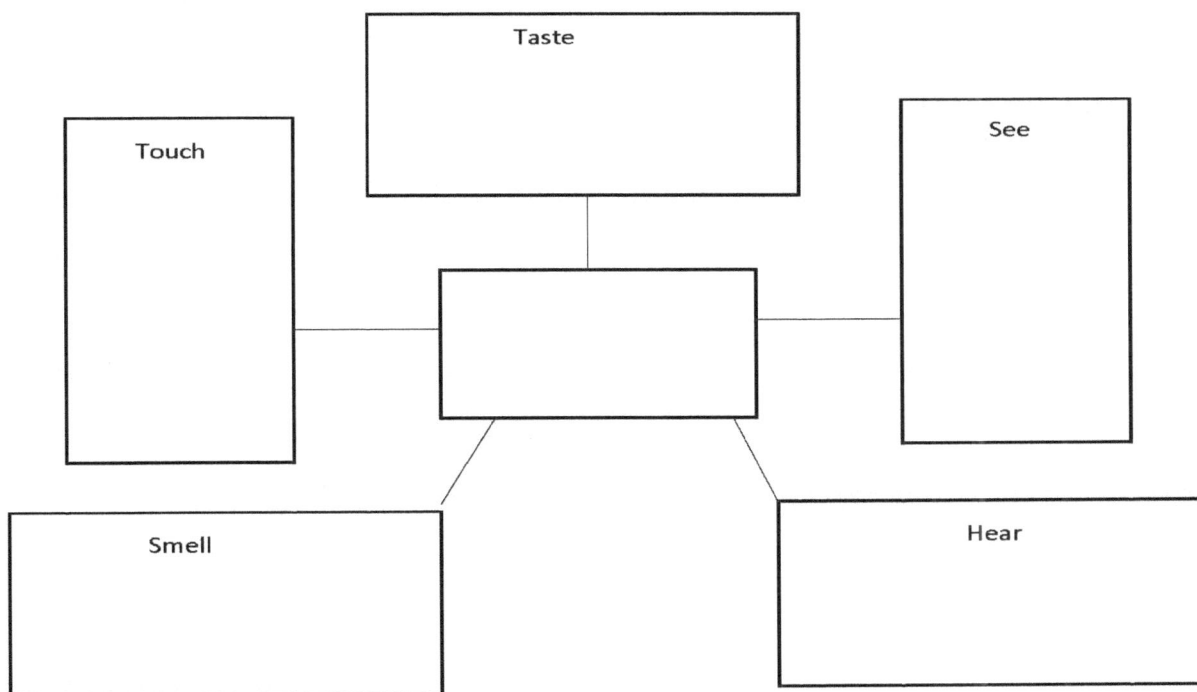

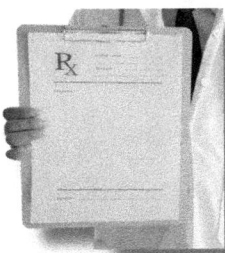

Taste

Touch

See

Smell

Hear

Brainstorming: *In the center box, write a word or phrase identifying the place and time you want to write about. (Examples: spring sunrise, winter snowstorm, bus station at night)*

Write the images in the blank space below in the order that creates the most clear or vivid impression of what you experienced.

List words and phrases describing what each of your senses are experiencing in this place and time.

Does anything you are sensing remind you of something else? Add it to your brainstorming.

Look back over your diagram. Circle or highlight the three strongest images.

Go over each line and add or remove words or syllables to create the correct number of beats. Example:

The orange sun is rises   5 syallables or beats

+Splashes bright pink and red   7 syllables or beats

+Against gray sky like a blank canvas   5 syllables or beats

Write a final copy of your haiku below.

_____

_____

_____

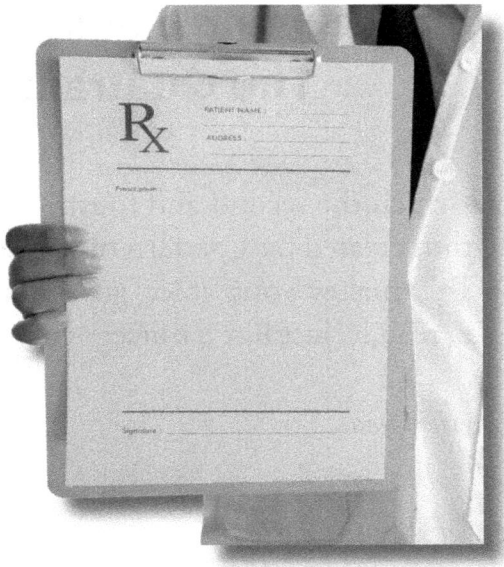

Rhyming Poems
The Couplet

Just as its name suggests, a couplet is two rhyming lines of poetry. A couplet can be a stand-alone poem, or you can write a series of related couplets, like those below, as stanzas for a longer poem.

My dog stands watch on the other side of the door,

His wagging tail thumping the floor.

He cares not if I am wealthy or smart,

But loves me still with all his heart.

If only man could be so good,

As to love whenever he should.

If a rhyming word doesn't quite fit, poets often use approximate rhyme (two words that sound very similar but don't exactly rhyme).

The girl stood, silent and alone

Waiting for the late bus home.

Rhyming Poems
The Quatrain

This is a four-line poem in which the second and fourth lines rhyme. It usually has a rhythm created by a pattern of stressed and unstressed syllables. This makes your voice go up and down in a pattern when you read it, just like a nursery rhyme.

He knelt beside the tiny bed
And held her small white hand
Watching as his child slipped
Into the Promised Land.

Brainstorming: *Choose a topic for your poem. This can be an incident or it could be a single moment in time. Write five to ten phrases or sentences about this topic in the space below.*

_____

_____

_____

_____

_____

_____

_____

_____

_____

Highlight or underline the strongest images and write them in a single sentence.

_____

_____

_____

Divide the sentence so that it fits the format of a couplet or quatrain. Remove unnecessary words.

_____

_____

_____

Rearrange or find synonyms for the ends of two lines to create a rhyme. The changed words should not interfere with the meaning or alter the mood or feel of the poem.

_____

_____

_____

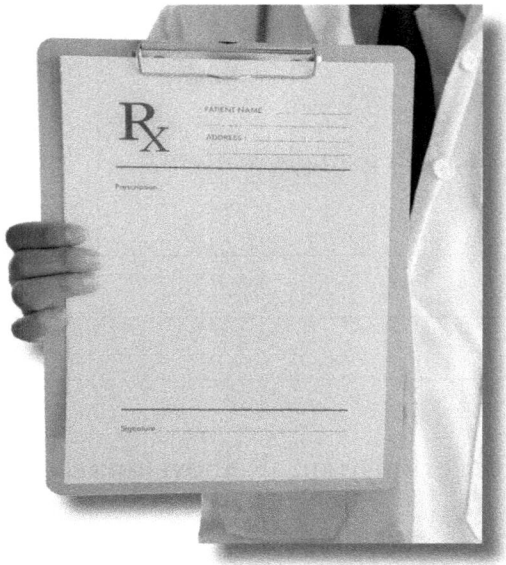

The Acrostic Poem

Rhyming or unrhyming, the acrostic gets its name from the fact that the first letter of each line, when read vertically, forms a word related to the poem's theme or topic.

Healing does not come at once, not here, he says

Only in fairytales where wizards work their magic

Patient suffering is the key to our survival

Even the dog knows that

Brainstorming: *Choose a word from the list below or come up with one of your own.*

- Trust
- Love
- Friendship
- Kindness
- Hope
- Joy
- Strength

Free-write for five minutes, listing words, phrases, and events from your own experience that describe or explain this word.

Writing: *Write your word vertically on the left end of the lines below. Add extra lines if needed.*

_____

_____

_____

_____

_____

_____

Go back to your free-write. Highlight or underline the strongest, most descriptive words and phrases.

Do any phrases or sentences naturally begin with one of the letters you have written on each line? If so, write them in. Then add words to your other phrases that will fit your remaining letters and add these to your poem.

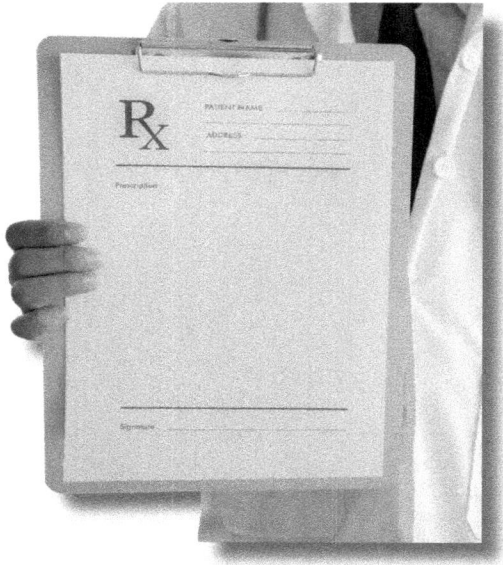

Free Verse

Free verse poems do not follow specific rules or rhyme schemes. They tend to focus on strong images to communicate larger concepts.

The cart overflows with remains

the leftovers of human life

that will not biodegrade

Refuse too good to waste

pushed down crowded city sidewalks

the treasure of a man

society threw away

Brainstorming: *Choose a topic from the list below or use one of your own.*

- Your first love
- A stranger you noticed in passing
- Your mother or father
- Your child at birth
- A character from a book you love
- Yourself of ten, twenty, or thirty years ago
- Yourself ten, twenty, or thirty years in the future

Visualize your topic. For five minutes, write down all the words and phrases you can to describe him/her. Think about what he/she looks like: hair, clothes, skin, posture, eyes, lips, nose, facial expression, attitude. Think about what he/she is doing: voice, tone, words, body movements, body language. What is this person's emotional state?

_____

_____

_____

_____

_____

_____

_____

_____

_____

Underline or highlight four or five of the most vivid and descriptive words and phrases. Number these in an order that will create the strongest image of the person.

Rewrite these phrases as a poem, adding or changing words to provide a more complete picture for your reader. Do not be concerned with rhyme, structure, or punctuation. Be concerned only with painting a picture of the person for your reader.

_____

_____

_____

_____

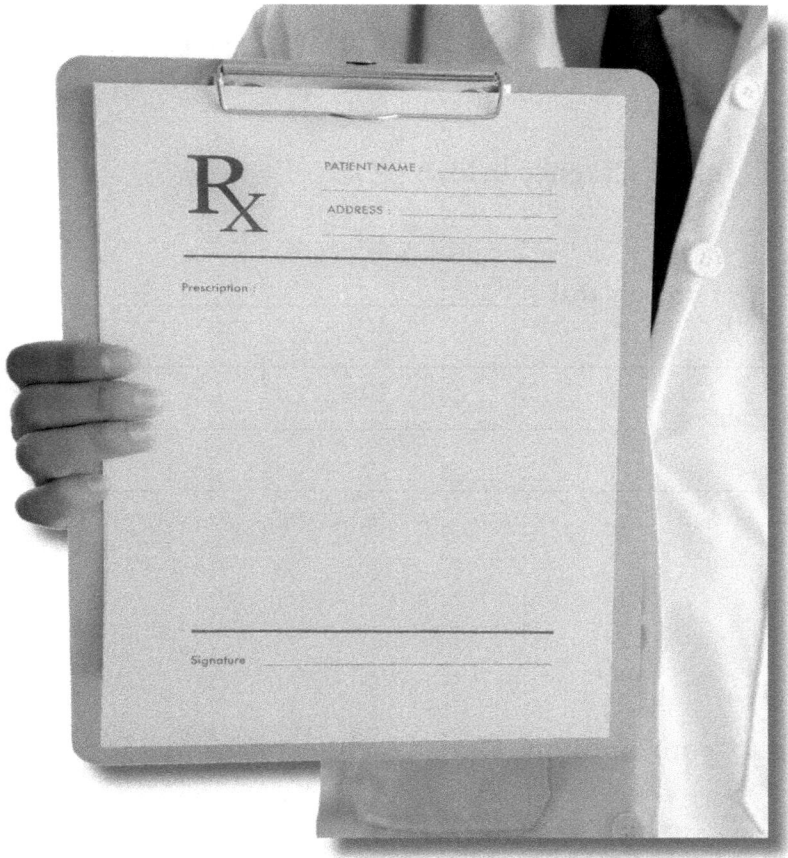

Essay

Opinion Essay

How-To Essay

Narrative Essay

Essays are pieces of writing that express a viewpoint, tell a story, or explain how to complete a task or master a skill. They are more structured than journal entries and are usually several paragraphs in length. They can be humorous or serious, personal or formal in tone. Essays as expressive writing can be helpful in identifying and solving a problem, expressing personal feelings, or understanding a situation by viewing it from a more objective perspective.

Opinion Essay

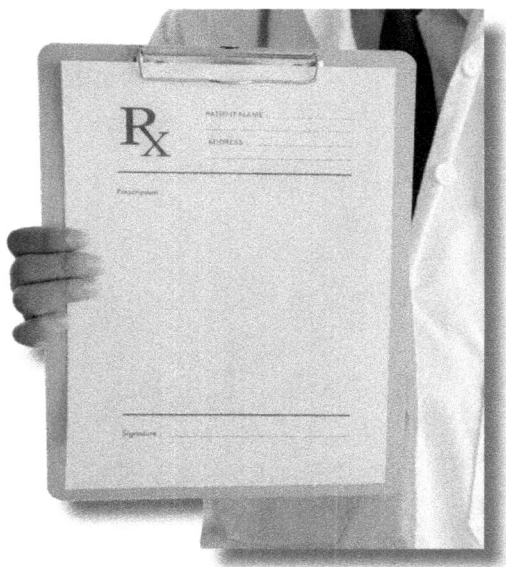

Fill in the sentence below:

I feel strongly that _____

_____

because _____

_____.

List three facts or examples that support your opinion. Under each, explain how it proves your opinion is valid.

Fact/Example 1_____

This proves my opinion is valid because

_____

_____

_____

_____

Fact/Example 2_____

This proves my opinion is valid because

_____

_____

_____

_____

Fact/Example 3_____

This proves my opinion is valid because

_____

_____

_____

_____

Briefly state one or two arguments someone on an opposing side might make to disprove your opinion.

_____

_____

_____

Is there anything valid in the opposing argument? If so, what can you offer to counterbalance that information?

_____

_____

_____

_____

_____

_____

_____

_____

_____

_____

_____

_____

_____

Writing: *Write one to three paragraphs using the ideas from your brainstorming. State your opinion and provide clear and logical support to explain why you feel the way you do. Consider how others might disagree and give reasons why their viewpoint is flawed or inaccurate. End with a strong and compelling restatement of your original opinion.*

_____

_____

_____

_____

_____

_____

_____

_____

_____

_____

_____

_____

_____

_____

_____

_____

_____

_____

_____

_____

_____

_____

_____

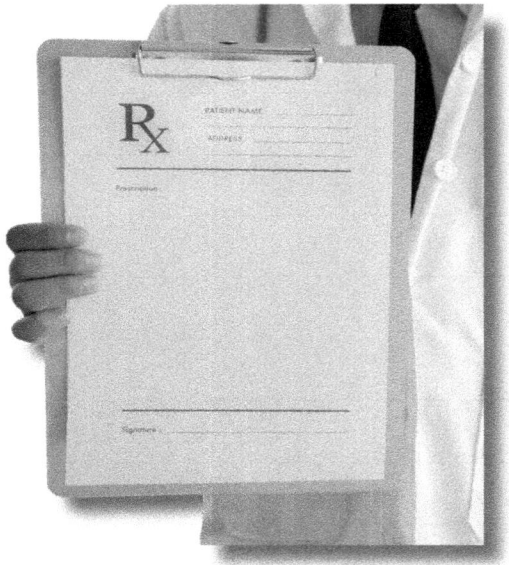

How-To Essay

Think about a skill, knowledge, or talent you have that could be useful to someone in your life or someone in a situation similar to your own. This can something you know or understand, like how to survive grief, how to be a better parent, or how to overcome an addiction. It can also be something you can physically do, like locating assistance as a veteran, undergoing treatment as a cancer patient, growing food for your family, or cooking like your grandmother.

Write one sentence summarizing what you will be explaining how to do in your essay.

_____

_____

_____

_____

_____

Who do you know who could benefit from this information? How do you hope it will help him/her?

_____

_____

_____

_____

_____

List any tools, materials, or prior knowledge that are necessary before your reader can apply what you are teaching him/her.

_____

_____

_____

_____

_____

Write out the steps you have followed to complete this task in the past. You can do this in a paragraph or in a numbered list. Use chronological order (in other words, the order in which the steps should be completed).

_____

_____

_____

_____

_____

_____

_____

_____

_____

_____

Read over what you wrote. Put a check next to steps that are clearly written. Put a question mark by any step that could be confusing. Ask yourself: Does it require more information? Would it be better to break this step into two parts?

Writing: *Write one to three paragraphs teaching your reader how to do something. Begin by explaining what the knowledge or skill is, and why it is important that you share it specifically with him/her. Provide information on any tools, materials, or prior knowledge your reader will need before starting the task. Give clear, easy-to-follow directions. End with encouragement, explaining what you hope he/she will gain by doing what you suggest.*

How To _____

_____

_____

_____

_____

_____

_____

_____

_____

_____

_____

_____

_____

_____

_____

_____

_____

_____

_____

_____

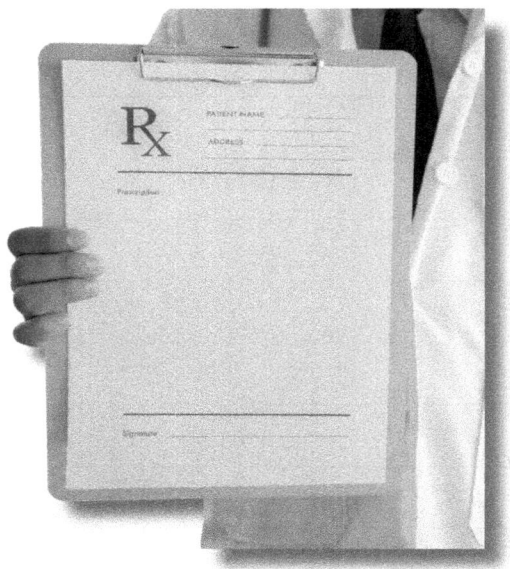

Narrative Essay

Think about an incident or event that was embarrassing, upsetting, or hurtful. In just one or two sentences, explain what happened.

_____

_____

_____

Now imagine that you can go back in time and watch this incident again, just as if it were a scene from a movie. No one can see you—you are just an observer. Use the Storyboard Diagram on the next page to fill in exactly what happens. Treat yourself as just another character, using the third person (your name or he/she/they instead of I and we).

Look over the Storyboard. Are there any additional details that you'd like to add that don't fit on the chart? Jot those down in the margins, or in the space below.

_____

_____

_____

_____

Storyboard Diagram

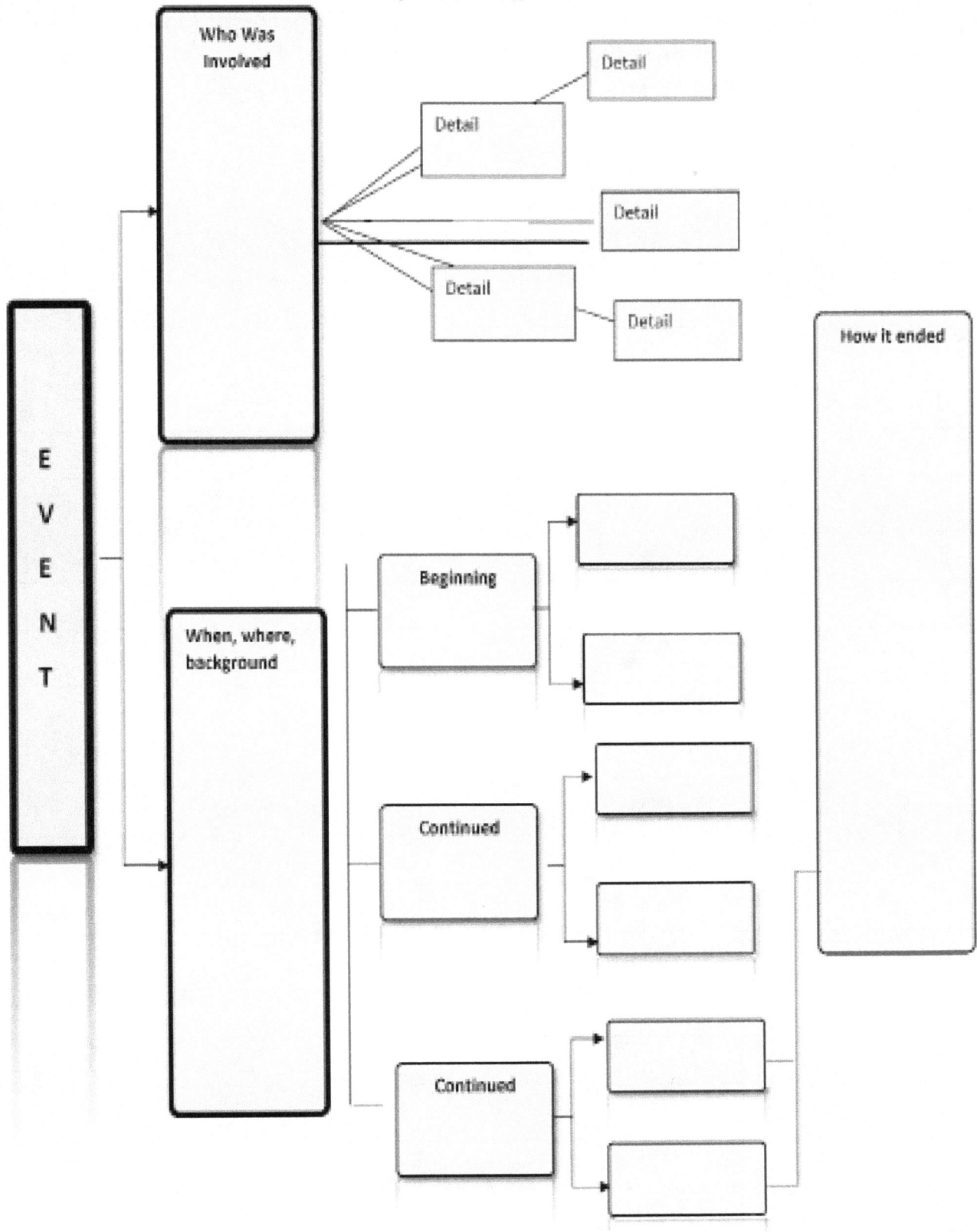

Writing: *Now write the story as it happened, in the third person. Where possible, try to imagine what other characters in the story were thinking and feeling rather than just focusing on your character. Include dialogue that is as close to the truth as you can remember. Strive to present every character and moment as honestly and objectively as possible.*

_____

_____

_____

_____

_____

_____

_____

_____

_____

_____

_____

_____

_____

_____

_____

_____

_____

_____

_____

_____

Read over your narrative. What new insights do you have about the event or the people involved?

_____

_____

_____

Do you see your own role in the same way as you did when you started?

_____

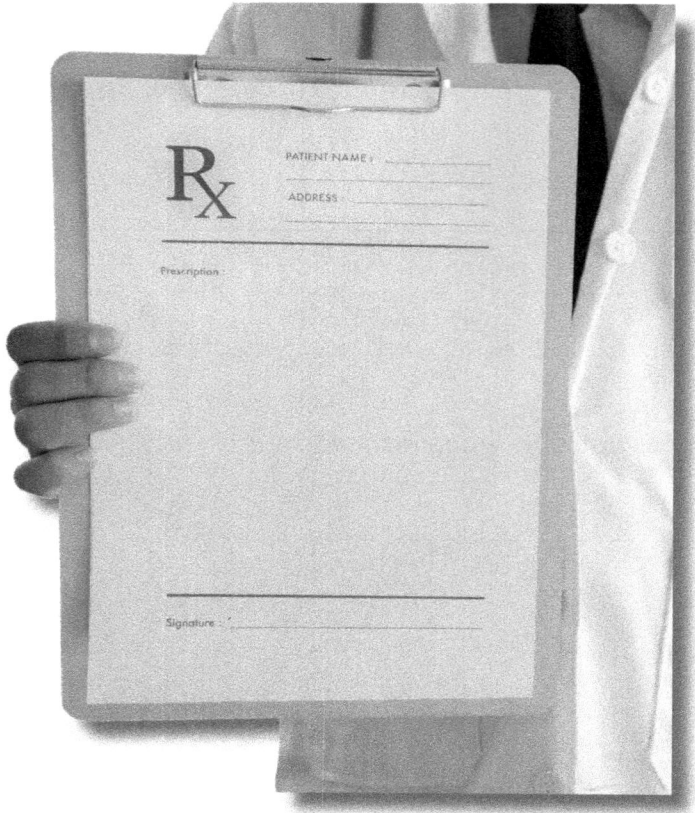

Reproducible Organizers

These blank organizers can be used to brainstorm for a variety of types of writing. They are reproducible for personal use.

Organizers

Comparison Contrast Diagram

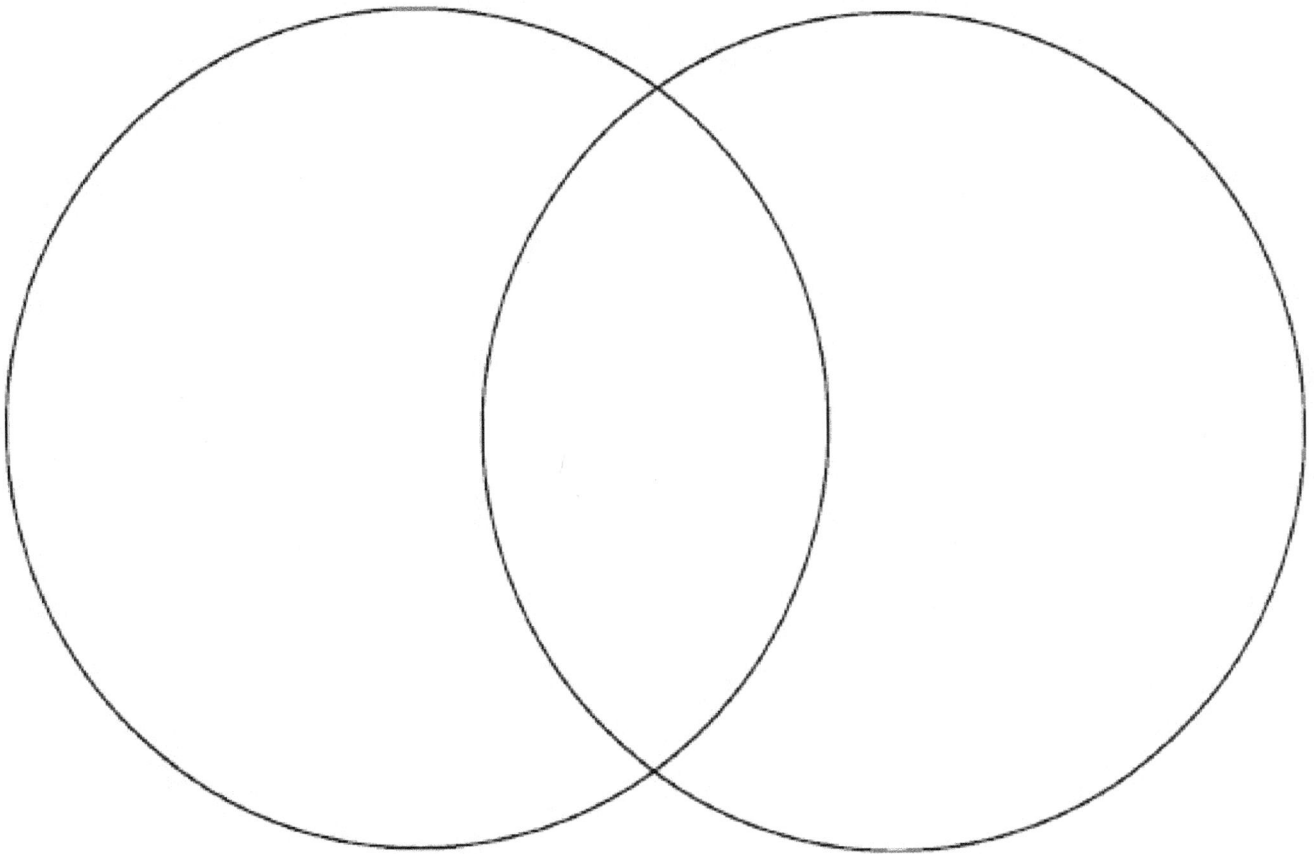

Organizers

Mental Map

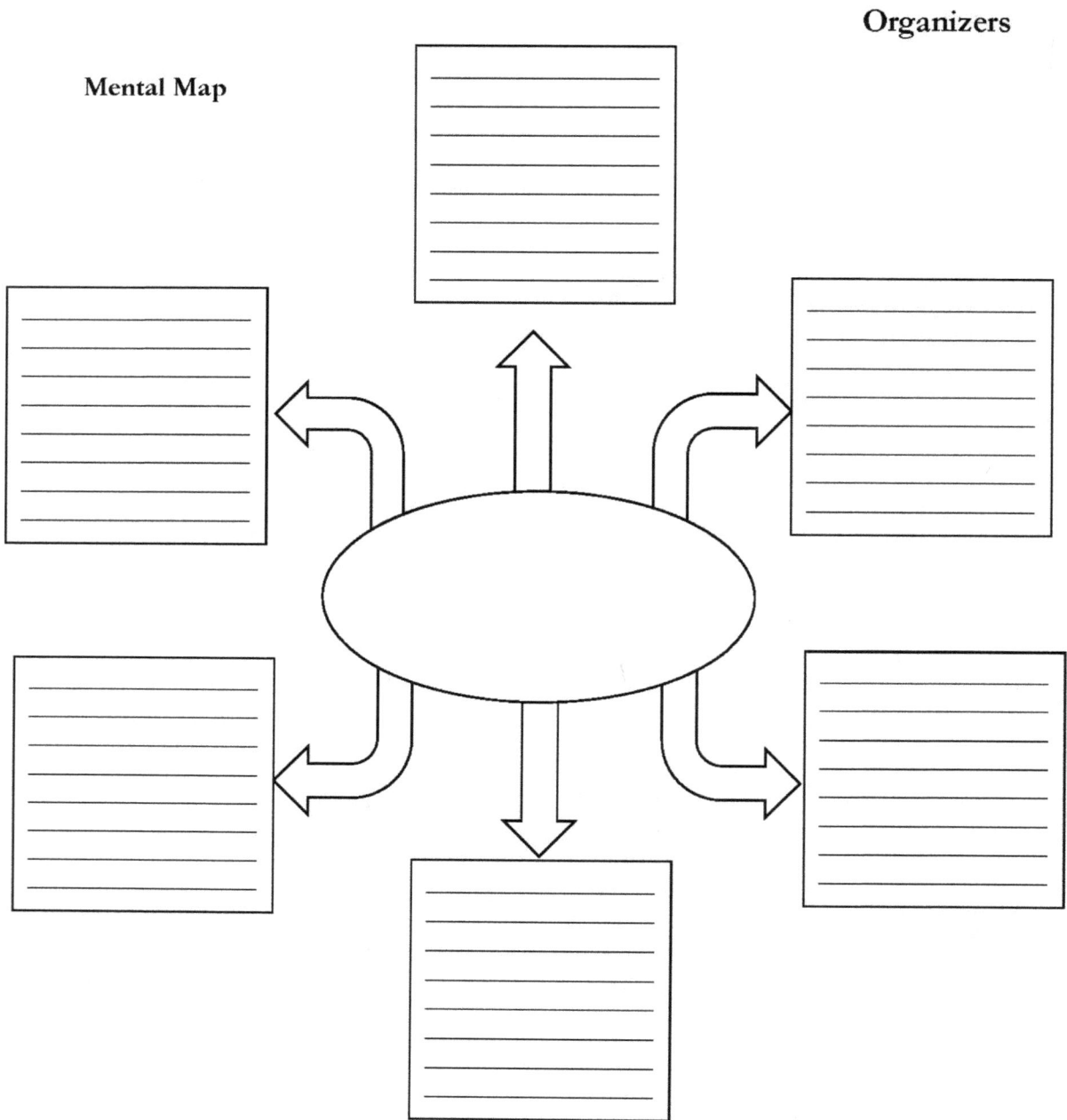

Organizers

Sensory Map

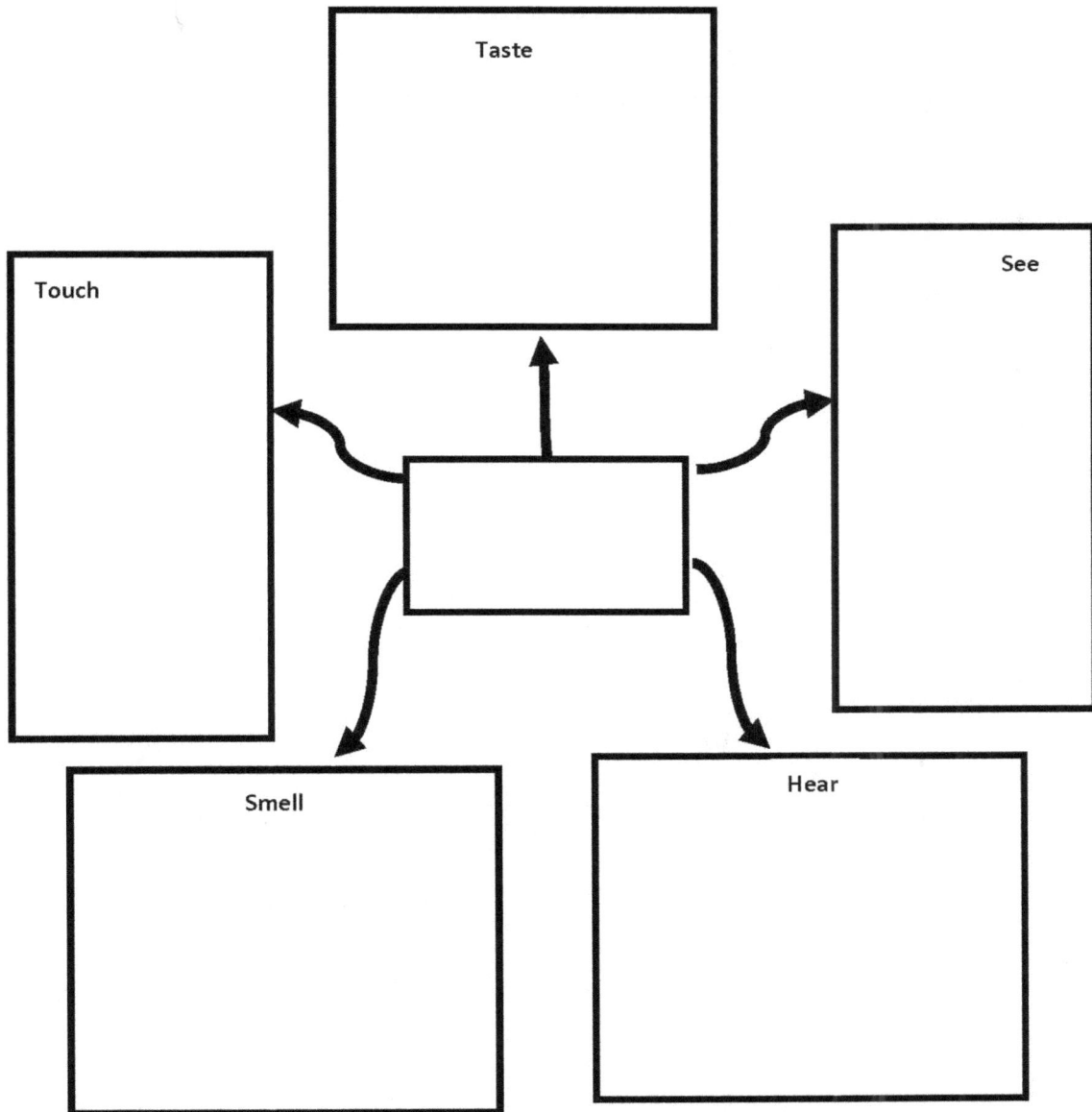

Storyboard Diagram

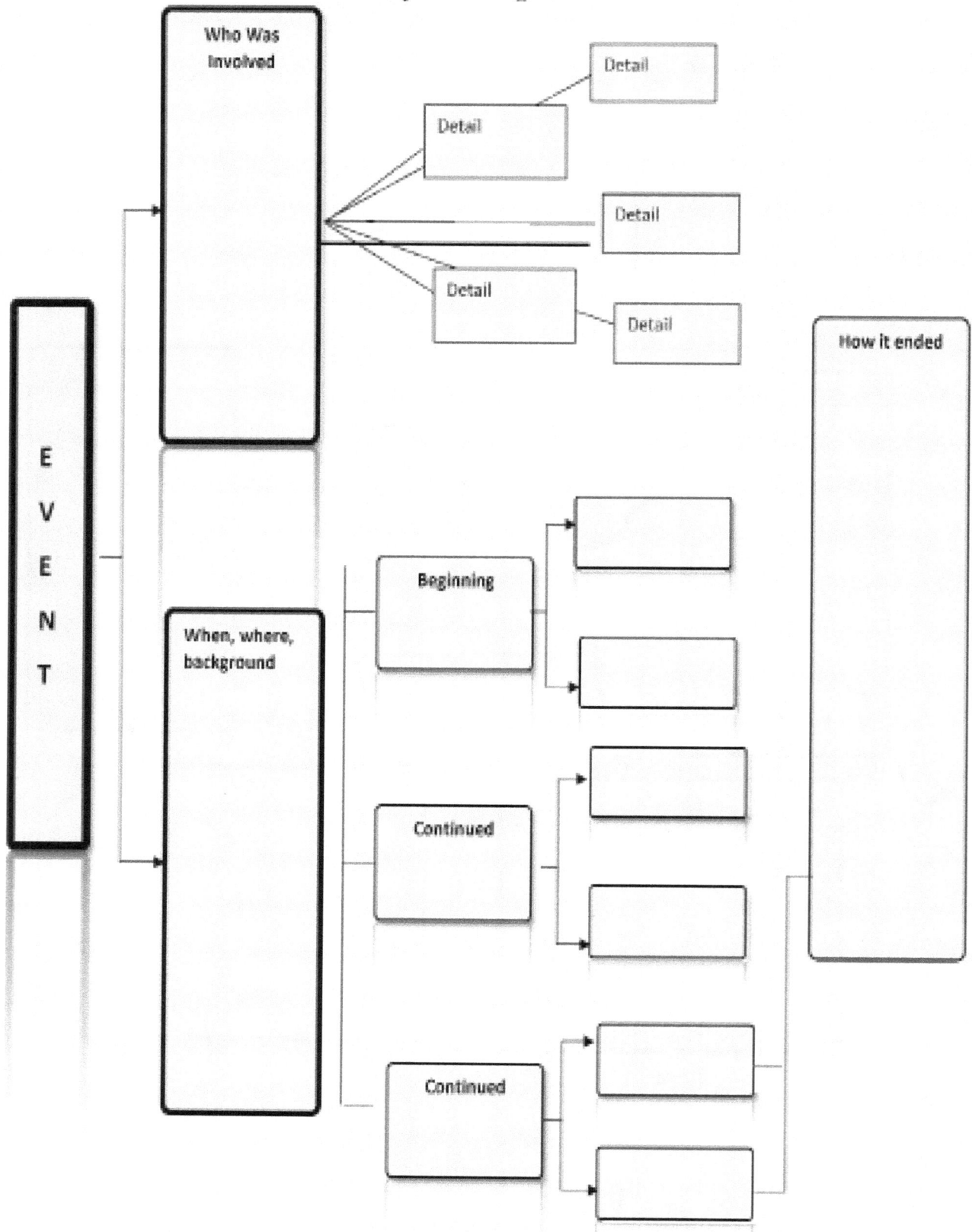

		Detail
	Detail	
		Detail
Who Was Involved	Detail	
		Detail
	Detail	

EVENT

When, where, background

Beginning

Continued

Continued

How it ended

About the Author

Ann Eichenmuller is an educator and outdoor recreation writer whose columns appear regularly in national and regional magazines. She is a two-time winner of *Boating Writers International Merit Awards* and the recipient of the *Washington Post's Agnes Meyer Award for Excellence in Education*. Ann is the author of two mystery novels, *Kind Lies* and *The Lies We Are*, as well as *The Writing Rx: Using the Healing Power of Writing for a Happier, Healthier Life*.

Something of an adventurer, she is a private pilot, avid boater, and certified diver whose favorite accomplishment is sailing with her husband and children to the Bahamas aboard their 33' Morgan Out Island.

Consider joining Ann's Facbook Group *The Writing Rx: Wellness through Journaling & Expressive Writing*. This is the link: https://www.facebook.com/groups/661810474150386

Ann's website is www.AnnEichenmuller.org